Thoughts Musings Dreams?

a book filled with my frappy thoughts.
Chill and have it with a sip of coffee :)

Tanushree Umesh Poojary

BookLeaf Publishing

India | USA | UK

Made with ❤ on the BookLeaf Publishing Platform
www.bookleafpub.in
www.bookleafpub.com

To Eesha, you are the light in my life

*Umesh, thanks for keeping me grounded and
being such a patient editor*

Hetansh and Divit, both of you are my superstars

*Thank you, Maa and Papa, for understanding
and tolerating my eccentrics :)*

*Thank you, Anna, Bhabhi, Mahesh, Shivli and
Snehal for your love and support*

*And thanks Mom, Dad and Nisha for
surrounding me with books and just for always
being there without asking*

Acknowledgement

Thank you BookLeaf Publishing for this unique opportunity to pen my thoughts in one place.

And to my family and friends—I am who I am because of you :)

Preface

Often I get so lost in the hum-drum life of my corporate career
That I forget how much I love to write, to think, and just to wonder, and let my thoughts wander!

This is my attempt to capture my ramblings and give some semblance to my creative thoughts.
Hope you enjoy reading it as much as I enjoyed writing it.

"I weave my dreams across your feet. Tread softly because you tread on my dreams"
—Byron

1. Radiance

Oh!
She shines so much
So bright,
It's like she sparkles
Maybe the sunlight graces upon her so gently
Maybe nothing can dull the glow from within

But why is she not aware of what she is?
Why does she let darkness surround her?
Why does she let it bewitch?
If only she knew
If only she knew
How beautiful she is
From outside and within.

2. The Last School Bell

Tick-Tock, Tick-Tock
It's like my ears yearn to hear the sound
I have some unquenchable thirst
Will it ring when I finally burst?

Doesn't this school understand
That time is so precious?
Especially when our minds are so keen
God knows so many places it has already been

We want to step out of these doors
Prance on our toes
Skip on those puddles
And whistle with the wind
Answer with our voices
Match with those honks of traffic

But look, the days stretch on like this—
From morning, and now it's almost evening
So ring, bell, ring!
Let me be me.

3. Sweet Shop

That heavenly smell is enough to lure me in
But when my feet head towards the threshold;
Those menacing eyes of the *halwai* are enough
to make me stop

In many streets,
You see me or pretend not to.
I go by the name
Ladka, Chokra, Bhikari, Street Urchin
These names
I have accepted with much dignity
As even I know
For most of the world
The clothes maketh the man

But when I close my eyes
And sleep at night
I dream of stepping out of a fancy car
looking suave in smart clothes
That fits like a glove.

In my dreams
I cross over that sacred threshold
And those menacing eyes are smiling at me
Asking me in a saccharine tone
"What will you have, beta?"
Like,
It was my birthright
I wish!
It was my birthright.

4. Grief

They say
Grief is intangible
Something with no shape
It can't be put in a container
Nor can be it touched
But only felt

But why is it
When I go through it
I get squashed
By this huge heavy wall
Closing in on me
Rendering me incapable of breathing

I have waves crashing in on me
Like I am caught in a never-ending tsunami
It glues my mouth and molds me into a statue
Completely paralyzed

And yet
They say grief is intangible
Something which can't be touched
Shouldn't have so much impact, yes?
Time heals all wounds and you will move on
But time doesn't heal *all* wounds
It just gives you the ability to pretend better
And the best pretender is called a sensible
adult

But yes
Grief is intangible
Even if it makes the air you breathe
Akin to broken glass shards.

5. Mumbai

I feel the minute you reach her
She welcomes you with open arms
Whether you were born here
or whether you are new
The city of dreams welcomes you

Such is the energy
Such is the buzz
You will see no one sitting idle
Every street, every locality
Streaming with people
Ready to just move

This city has mansions where the uber-rich
reside
And yet in the same amount of space as those
palaces
Many struggling poor clam up and make their
home

There is no dearth of multi-cuisine high-end
restaurants
But there is also always vada pav
To welcome you with a smile

Despite the chaos, dirt, traffic and the
pollution
There are many who lose their heart to the
city every day
The traffic makes it hard to move
But that's the city's way of
Making you stop and think

The average homes in Mumbai may be small
But the hearts are so so big
We have all seen 26/06 and 26/11—
Dark days, yet the spirit of Mumbai
For the people and by the people still stood

Tourists from outside the city say the air
stinks
But where else can you see such vibrancy,
such variety
The vibe, the feel which lets you dream and
gives you the drive
to fulfill your dreams

Toast to the chaats of Ghatkopar
To the fabulous street shopping of Bandra
To the busy streets of Andheri
To the corporates of Malad
To the natural beauty of Arrey
To my IT bros in Powai
And above all, toast to this city
That many millions call home

I am lucky it's the city of my birth
I had moved away for two decades
And yet once I got back
It's like I was never gone at all
So yes I am lucky it's the city of birth
and proud it will be my city of death.

6. My Daughter

When I first saw her
I remember the exact moment
My life—so dull and dark
Suddenly painted with so many vibrant colors

Before I had her I thought I knew everything
But now I never cease to learn
She is a constant wonder
Her prattling, her queries, her stories

Even when she throws tantrums
I can't stop being amazed at her
We make each other angry
But we can't be without each other

When I scold her
It hurts me the most
When she gets hurt
My heart stops for a moment
Her smile brings the dawn of the day
And when she sleeps
It's like everything else ceases to exist

Her quest to find knowledge is relentless
Her curiosity knows no boundaries
And yet I know when I am feeling down
In her, I feel my stability

To me, she is the most beautiful girl in the
world
To her, sometimes I am just her annoying
irritating mother
But every moment without her is pointless
And I am lucky she chose me to be her
mumma

One day
She will grow up
Move on
And fled the nest
But I know
She will always know
How much her parents and family love her.

7. My Husband

Tall as a gentle oak he is
Quiet unassumingly he walks into the room
A man of a few words
Introspective and inquisitive
But his words once uttered command all
attention

Strong-willed fiery tempered
Yet a tender soul and a good listener
Witty, intelligent, he is immensely
detail-oriented
He seems tough to others, but I know he is
just like a coconut

He is a man of action
Who does all the work behind the scenes
Without taking any credit
Yet his accomplishments shine through

He is a strong shoulder to lean on
And the go-to person when there is a need to
make serious decisions
And yet he is also the one to come up with
such lame jokes which are
Sometimes beyond my comprehension
And the cause of great irritation

A great parent, a good friend
A wonderful human being
A quick conversationalist
And even when he thinks he falters
To me, even then he shines

I am fortunate to have him by my side
As a guide
As my compass.

8. Purpose

What is my purpose in this life?
This question might pop up in our minds at
one point or the other
Who decides this purpose?
And once decided, who gives society the right
to determine
If it is optimal or not for us
To judge us if they feel it is not apt for us

To a homemaker, taking care of the home or
family might be fulfilling
To a corporate individual the hustle-bustle of
the paper chase might make it complete
To each their own.

We all have our own map to follow,
Our own choices to make
Our own decisions to follow which makes us
very much us

If something as basic as two smartphones
Can be so customized
Then how do we expect someone as complex
As a human being to be the same
It's not like we are cut out of the same cloth

Maybe if we stop making it our purpose to
gain validation from others
And do the things that actually make us
happy
We would gain our real purpose in life.

9. Logic Versus Creative Brain

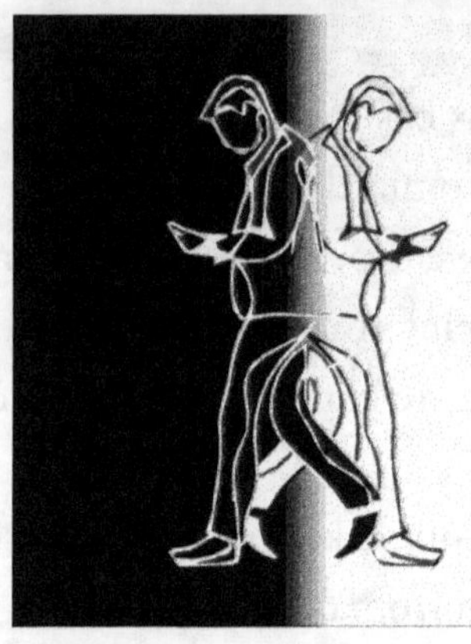

Whenever I feel that I should sing aloud
Or dance or write something down
There is that nagging feeling rising
from within me
You know that annoying voice telling me:

Don't you have some actual work to do?
Yes, the one currently paying your bills
The one where you actually have to use your
brain
The work where everything falls in line

Where all the zeros and ones add up
Where one plus one equals two
Where the computer, day in and day out
Only does what you tell it to do
Where everything is simple
There is no room for emotions

'Cause emotions complicate matters
Emotions distract
But oh emotions fuel the creative brain
They surely inspire the greatest work
With them around, life is no more than
one-dimensional

But scoot away, says the logical brain again
We don't have time to waste away
The work you and I have to do is monumental
And all this creative brain wants to do is have
a siesta
'Pfft'

And so the tussle goes on and on!

10. The one who left us behind

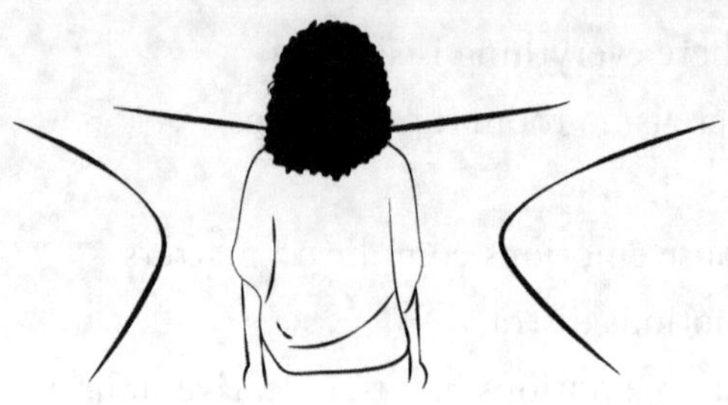

I wonder when they leave
Don't they think about the ones that are left
behind?
The ones who recall all their memories
Holding on to them like their most prized
possession

The burden is deep
For the ones who are left behind
Because even if their memory may fail
They try to remember every word of the last
conversation
They ever had

Thinking of the ones who have gone away
They wonder if they had spoken about how
much they love them
How much they miss them
Whether they had hugged or kissed them one
last time
Apologized for ever taking them for granted

With such a heavy load of emotions on their
shoulders
With so much lost, unsaid and unheard
Even time holds still waiting for them to
come back
Yet they simply step away
Leaving everything behind.

11. Greece

I still remember the moment the plane
touched down
The sight of the dazzling azure Ionian Sea
Basking in all its glory
Was the country of my dreams

Our first stop was Athens
Seemingly covered with a layer of dust
Its every stone, every building seemed to tell a
story
Hushed with time and of the centuries gone
by

The hike to the Acropolis and Lycabettus hill
With its bird's-eye vantage view of the
glorified city
The hushed archaic beauty of the city
churches
The decorated stature of the Pynx which
spoke about democracy
and its birth in hushed reverence

The charming beauty of Syntagma Square
among the city buzz
The miniature orange trees in all its bloom
Spreading fragrance around the city
All filled me with immense joy
Which were gladly tucked away in my
Treasure box of cherished memories

Our next stop was Santorini
The jewel of the Ionian Sea
Every sight of it was so picturesque
No camera could capture its beauty

The fiery black and red beaches
The pearl and sapphire buildings of Oia,
Santorini
Which dazzled during the day and glowed at
sunset

The sight of the sunrise and the sunset
And those fabulous olives, honey and yoghurt
Those sweet little indulgences

Just thinking about it makes me
Want to go back
So we can bask in the Greek sunlight
Tell tall tales like we used to
And just linger
Taking all that beauty in!

12. My favorite season

As someone who grew up in the equator
(Singapore)
I missed having four seasons
So imagine my joy when we moved back to
the homeland
Where there is happiness in every season

Although in a coastal city like Mumbai
The humidity and sea air make the weather
tepid
My favorite season is still winter
Although in Mumbai it would mostly reach a
minimum of 20 degrees

Winter has its charm
There is crispiness in the air
It smells of Christmas cookies
And wondrous whispers of celebrations
And a year gone by well

Winter doesn't have the stickiness of summer
The chaos and change of fall
But the solid stability knowing if all else fails
It's the season of hibernation

I like cuddling in my hot blanket
Sipping hot chocolate
Baking festive cookies
And singing aloud carols

I like recalling all the memories
of the past year
And catching up with friends and family

But mostly, I like just the cool pleasantness of
the air
Tingling my senses, lulling me
Making me happy and putting me at ease.

13. Heart Break

What is heartbreak?
It is like a slow paralytic poison which seeps
into you
Letting you breathe but paralyzing you in its
grip

It is in our human nature to desire happiness
To want love, to desire love
No matter how dire or hopeless our situation
might be
But as Newton once said
Every action has an equal and opposite
reaction
So if we are ready to experience love
We should be ready to experience heartbreak,
shouldn't we?

But what can prepare you for this
Gut-wrenching, earth-shattering pain
Which makes you want to pull the covers over
your head
Which makes you relive every moment your
heart broke
in vivid clarity

Why is it that when you are down
Your brain comes up with more memories
That are likely to make you more upset
It's not like we cherish our own pain
Or we are sadistic enough to gloat in our own
sorrow

But that's the way we deal
We comprehend what makes us upset
And thinking about those times
When we wallow
It helps us open those locks
We have placed in our mind
And helps us heal better

With every heartbreak, every hurt
Yes, we drown
But when we surface, we emerge stronger
Because yes, what doesn't kill us
Does make us stronger
And also teaches us lessons about ourselves.

14. Singapore

We all have a biased love for our birth
country
But I am lucky, because I received the love of
not only the country of my birth
But also the country which has raised me

I have spent twenty years of my life
On a sunny island where east to west can be
traversed in an hour
I have seen people of all diversity
Living in such equality
Where Chinese New Year and Diwali were
celebrated among friends
With equal amount of gusto

Where, when I was hungry
I knew I could count on having Hainanese
fried rice, Biriyani and Satay
Among my options
Where, although it was hot and humid all day
The cool air-conditioned shopping center air
Was always there welcoming everywhere

I thrived on window shopping with my
friends
Long walks in the park
Long talks on the phone
Barbequing during the summer holidays
Talking crap to each other while sitting on
the bus and train

Our thing was always
Catching the latest movies in Golden Village
or Cathay
Queuing for every small or big thing
Because that was the way

For me being in Singapore also included
going to the temple
Or visiting Little India with my parents
Rushing off to my classes, studies or project
work in school or college
And lastly, dashing off to work in the middle
of the country

Singapore is where my heart was broken,
mended
Also where I found my forever love
And before I knew it, my time was up
And I had to leave behind the country I once
called home.

15. Temple

Whenever I am down or feel uneasy
There is no place I feel like going
Other than the nearest place of worship

Just entering the sacred sanctuary
Fills my mind with inner peace
I feel like I get dispelled of all negativities
By reaching up and pushing the temple bell

Chanting the prayers and sitting on the cool
floor
Puts my anxious heart to rest
Resting on the pillars of the temple
Is my one true solace

Many may go to the temple to pray
But I go there sometimes just to sit
Open my mind
And find my inner peace.

16. Fur babies

Even before I learned to love my siblings,
friends,
Special friends or maybe my husband
I had a special kind of love
For my dog and my cat—
For these two were my lovely fur babies

They filled my life with laughter and wonder
Through their display of unconditional love
My heart used to fill with joy
When they waited for me to come home
My whole day would feel complete

Their mischief makes me amused
And them messing up the house is annoying
But nothing used to make me feel more
serene
Than cuddling up with my fur babies

When they left me and went to their heavenly
abode
Although I was very heartbroken,
grief-stricken, and upset
I felt better knowing that
One day, when all is said and done
I will meet them again when I cross the
rainbow bridge.

17. Siblings

When we first came into this world
In our family, our first friends came to us
naturally
They are what everyone terms as our siblings.

As much as they bickered with us
Whenever we needed someone to pick up the
pieces for us
They were there
Though they were the first ones to tattle to
the parents
They also safeguarded us from them when
things became too grim

They shared everything with us
From toys to books
To the little pockets of joy and the burden of
our sorrow

They humbled us by relating to us and
listening to us
They gave us serious life lessons, told us bad
jokes
And held our hand or hair when we had our
first heartbreak or hangover
or our first brush of grief

So even though now as adults
Some of us may not contact our siblings daily
But we know somewhere
That they would always have our back.

18. College Life

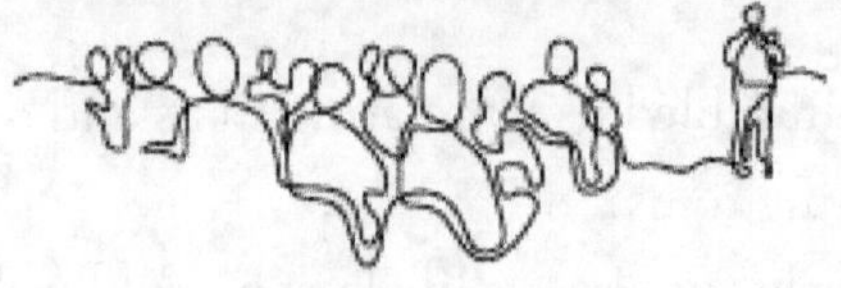

College comes at a time
When we are going through
One of the most transitionary phases of our
life

From the precipice of our childhood
The last hoorays of our teenage years
We step into this educational institute
Where we don't have to wear a uniform
anymore

We not only have to select our own clothes
But also have to forge new friendships
Some of us are lucky if our old friends from
school have followed us to the same college
But for most of us, it is a very shaky start

And on top of everything that is going on,
there are lectures to attend
So much content to cram
The projects and assignments to finish, and
exams to prepare for

But who doesn't remember, from their college
days
The on-the-spur gossip sessions with friends
The canteen hangouts between lectures
The banter pulling each other's legs and the
support during the long days
The shopping quests to find the latest fashion
in thrift

The time spent in college felt too short
As I felt I had my first lessons in the real
world— in survival, love, friendship, dealing
with time,
people and situations toxic or otherwise
In such a compact time
the time spent during college
Will always be etched in my heart.

19. First job apprehension

On the downtrodden days, when the world
was reeling from the effects of the subprime
mortgage crisis
I stepped out from the comfort of my
university
Into the jaws of the real world to clamber
into my job search
Possibly in the banking or financial domain
I was full of self-doubts and fear
The search even felt fruitless
It feels like my day would start with sending
out countless resumes everywhere
And waiting for someone to call me

Finally after 6 months of this depressing
mind-numbing cycle
I found a job where I felt my skills and
education were well-utilized
But a different sense of foreboding set in

What should I wear on my first day of work?
What if I am not able to carry out the
responsibilities of the job?
What if my colleagues are not friendly?
What if there isn't anyone to mentor me?
What if? What if? What if?
With all these what-ifs in my mind, I forayed
into my job
Only to be welcomed and welcomed well
My first job has also given me what we term
now as *experience*
Which counts as a solid rung in my corporate
career.

20. Anxiety

Of all the emotions one can feel
Nothing is as awful as this feeling—
That sinking or dragging sensation that pulls
you down
Making you constantly look over your
shoulder

Having you second-guess or third-guess every
single decision
And fighting this constant battle to keep
calm
Like your life depended on it

But what makes this feeling worse
Is that nothing seems right and everything
only becomes more ominous
Everyone feels it at one point or the other in
their life

It's like pinpricks on the skin
It's like dread slowly coming in
It's akin to a sunny day with a total eclipse
occurring
And bringing in complete darkness
It's like wanting to ram into a hard surface,
just to find an outlet

But what makes anxiety so despairing is that
We often give it the right to make us feel
Like we are anything other than the average
human being
That we pretend to be.

21. Traffic jam

Honk! The cars blast at each other
As if reminding one another of their
importance
Although in one line branching off
Trying to get by each other

Hey! Give way, the cars clash
The tires seem to screech at each other
Don't you know I have somewhere to go?
With a higher priority than you
Guzzling fumes at each other
And even the pedestrians
Slowly poisoning the environment

The halting sound of the ambulance
Breaks the car out of their reverie
All the cars begrudgingly hustle away
Suddenly they are reminded
Although their work is important
Nothing is as pertinent as the value of human
life

And then the ambulance goes by
And everything goes back to ground zero
Again they are trying to sidestep each other
To be the number one on the road!

22. Jupiter

As a child growing up, I had a fascination
with space
And this became stronger and stronger
Until every single book and news on space
was devoured
Soon all these musings led me to a different
trajectory where
I would dream of building a rocket

Which would whisk me away to the cosmos
I would fly whizzing past the meteoroids and
comets
Past all those planets to my favorite one
In my trusty neon-green futuristic spacecraft
In, of course, lightning speed

What is my favorite planet you ask!
Why, of course, the murky, elusive Jupiter
The largest planet in the solar system
With so many moons gravitating around it
A storm brewing on it for about 300 years
Which is as strong as the storm brewing
inside me

In my dreams, I revel in it
I can dance in the eye of the storm
I feel my hair flying everywhere and
Then something goes completely wrong

An alien comes out of nowhere
Oh no! It looks like my clone
I call upon my snazzy spaceship for rescue
But I find it already gone!

I start panicking and my stomach is rumbling
I do some grumbling
Thank god, the alarm then rings
Reality sets in and I am actually again back
home.

23. Motherhood

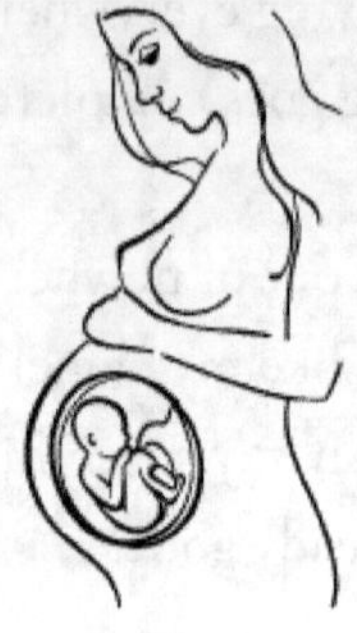

When you give birth to a child
The child also gives birth to a mother
A complex being who gets overjoyed
At the happiness of her offspring
Also known to cry at the drop of a hat
When overwhelmed by emotions

Sometimes a nurturer, sometimes the child's
first teacher
Other times a friend or simply a companion
When the child hurts, their heart bleeds
When the child errs, they feel guilt
When the child does well and makes them
proud
They shine even brighter with glory

Her days are spent gravitating around her
child
Her nights are spent in their worries
A "without pay" thankless job daily
Without any leaves or vacation days

When she is a stay-at-home mom
They say she overindulges
And doesn't she have her own individuality?
But when she goes out to work
They say she is selfish
And doesn't she care about her child?

Two sides of the same coin
Two sides of the same guilt
And yet, all is forgiven
And all is reset
At the sight of the smile on her child's face
This is motherhood...